COSORI Air Fryer Cookbook for Beginners

Quick and Foolproof COSORI Air Fryer Recipes For Your Whole Family with Beginner's Guide

By Linda Cook

Copyright © 2019 by Linda Cook

All rights reserved.

This document is geared towards providing exact and reliable information in regard to the topic and issue covered. The publication is sold with the idea that the publisher is not required to render accounting, officially permitted, or otherwise, qualified services. If advice is necessary, legal or professional, a practiced individual in the profession should be ordered.

From a Declaration of Principles which was accepted and approved equally by a Committee of the American Bar Association and a Committee of Publishers and Associations.
In no way is it legal to reproduce, duplicate, or transmit any part of this document in either electronic means or in printed format. Recording of this publication is strictly prohibited and any storage of this document is not allowed unless with written permission from the publisher. All rights reserved.

The information provided herein is stated to be truthful and consistent, in that any liability, in terms of inattention or otherwise, by any usage or abuse of any policies, processes, or directions contained within is the solitary and utter responsibility of the recipient reader. Under no circumstances will any legal responsibility or blame be held against the publisher for any reparation, damages, or monetary loss due to the information herein, either directly or indirectly. Respective authors own all copyrights not held by the publisher.

Table of Contents

Introduction 1

Chapter 1: What Your COSORI Premium Air Fryer Can Do 2
The Features of COSORI Air Fryer 4
Limitations of The COSORI Air Fryer 6

Chapter 2: General Instructions When Using Your COSORI Air Fryer 8
Using the Preset Air Frying Programs 10
How to Do Manual Air Frying 12
General Safety Instructions 12
COSORI Air Fryer Troubleshooting Guide 14

Chapter 3: Breakfast & Brunch Recipes 16
Coconut Milk, Egg 'n Spinach Casserole 16
Bell Pepper, Beef & Egg Scramble 17
Spanish Rice Casserole with Cheesy Beef 18
Marinara Sauce Over Cheesy Eggplant Bake 20
Garlic 'n Sour Cream Zucchini Bake 22
Smoked Trout Frittata 23
Bacon-Spinach Egg Cups 24
Chives, Coconut Cream & Mushroom Quiche 25
Zucchini 'n Chorizo Frittata 26
Creamy Ham 'n Egg Casserole 27
Garlic Beef & Egg Brekky Frittata 28
Creamy Mushroom-Egg Bake 29

Chapter 4: Appetizers & Sides Recipes 30

    Paprika, Garlic 'n Onion Rubbed Chicken Strips 30

    Crispy Fried Chicken Breasts Buffalo Style 32

    Zucchini Garlic Fries 34

    Paprika 'n Cajun Seasoned Onion Rings 35

    Crab Cakes Seasoned with Old Bay 'n Dijon 36

    Coconut Shrimps with Pina Colada Dip 37

    Crispy Paprika-Fish Nuggets 39

    Buffalo Chicken Dip 40

Chapter 5: Poultry Recipes 41

    Garlic Rosemary Roasted Cornish Hen 41

    Ginger-Garam Masala Rubbed Chicken 42

    Delicious Chicken Cordon Bleu 43

    Southern Style Fried Chicken 44

    Chicken Marinated in Coconut Milk with Ginger-Cilantro 45

    Turkey Meatballs in Cranberry Sauce 46

    Creamy Chicken Breasts Bake 47

    Hearty Chicken Potpie 48

    Butter-Lemon on Chicken Thighs 49

    Garlicky-Dijon Chicken Thighs 50

Chapter 6: Beef, Pork and Lamb Recipes 51

    Honey-Balsamic Sauce on Roast Beef 51

    Homemade Corned Beef with Onions 52

Southwestern Meaty Pasta Bake 53

BBQ Memphis Pork Ribs 55

Chinese Salt and Pepper Pork 56

Spicy Breaded Air Fried Pork Chops 57

Grilled Beef with Soy-Daikon Sauce 58

Sage 'n Thyme Rubbed Porterhouse 59

Cheesy-Bacon Stuffed Pastry Pie 60

Sweet 'n Sour Glazed Meatloaf 61

Jambalaya with Shrimps 'n Sausage 63

Mexican Rice 'n Sausage Bake 65

Cheesy Bacon Burger Casserole 66

Mouthwatering Beef Potpie Recipe 68

Chapter 7: Vegan and Vegetarian Recipes 69

Seasoned Veggie Wontons 69

Veggie Burger with Spice Medley 71

Bell Pepper-Mushroom Pizza 72

Creamy Baked Potato with Olives 73

Middle Eastern Falafel Recipe 74

Garlicky Kale-Potato Nuggets 75

Milky-Sauce on Cauliflower Steak 76

Pesto-Cream Cheese Stuffed Mushrooms 77

Cheesy-Bacon Stuffed Jalapeno 78

Easy-Peasy Balsamic Brussels Sprouts 79

Chapter 8: Desserts Recipes 80

Mouthwatering Blackberry Cobbler 80

Blueberry-Lemon Cake 82

Garlic-Parmesan Knots 83

Tasty Peach Pies... 84

Churros with Choco Dip... 85

Salted Pistachios on Brownies... 87

Introduction

With so many diseases related to eating fatty foods, it is no wonder why kitchen appliances such as ovens and indoor grills are popular. While broiled and grilled foods are great, nothing can beat the satiating feeling that fried foods can give. But what if I tell you that you can enjoy guilt-free fried foods at the comfort of your home?

There is no magic involved in making guilt-free fried foods at home. All it takes is ingenuity and the right kitchen equipment. This is where the nifty air fryer comes in. Designed to allow you to cook guilt-free fried food, the COSORI Air Fryer is not just an ordinary air fryer. In fact, it can be considered as the apex in all premium air fryers sold in the market today because of its many features.

Unlike other air fryers that allow you to cook almost the same thing every day, the COSORI Air Fryer will allow you to make different kinds of food aside from your favorite fries and chicken. Thus, let this book serve as your guide when it comes to using your COSORI Air Fryer and be amazed at the many things that you can make out of this nifty kitchen appliance. Read on!

Chapter 1: What Your COSORI Premium Air Fryer Can Do

The COSORI Air Fryer is designed in California and is designed to fit the aesthetics and space of any American kitchen. Unlike other air fryers that you have ever seen. While other air fryers allow you to cook only your fried favorites, this air fryer is designed so that you can also use to create all sorts of food from your favorite fries to bread. Below are the benefits that your COSORI Air Fryer can give you.

COSORI AIR FRYER

- **Make healthier fried foods:** This air fryer allows you to use 85% less fat compared with traditional fryers using its Air Crisp Technology. Although you will use less oil, you will still be able to make delicious and crunchy fried foods that you will truly enjoy. Moreover, unlike other air fryers that require you to brush or slather your food with oil, the COSORI Air Fryer only requires you to mist your food with just a tiny amount of oil to get the same effects as with conventional fried foods.

- **Make different kinds of food:** You are not limited to making fried foods with this particular air fryer. You can bake, roast, and even grill meats inside the large air fryer basket. There is no limit on what you can make with this air fryer. Aside from your usual crispy fried chicken, you can also enjoy pizza, steak, and even cakes using this air fryer.

- **Easy to use and saves you a lot of time:** Using conventional fryers can be tough because you have to always be there in front of the fryer to make sure that your food does not burn. With the COSORI Air Fryer, it has a built-in digital menu with 11 preset cooking setting so that you can cook like a pro. All there is to it is to put your food in the fryer tray and leave it until it cooks. It provides an easy and convenient way of cooking fried foods so that you can also attend to other important things in the kitchen.

- **Faster cooking time:** Faster cooking time means that you and your family can eat your favorite fried foods faster than conventional frying methods. Although you cook your food faster, you still get crispier and more delicious foods without worrying that your food will burn.

- **Safe to use:** The COSORI Air Fryer is FDA and ETL certified and it comes with an automatic shutoff to prevent overheating and overcooking of food. When it comes to safety to the health, the air fryer is BPA-free and PFOA-free. It also comes with a cool touch handle as well as a button guard to prevent detaching it accidentally. This will make you feel at ease knowing that this kitchen appliance is safe to use even for kitchen newbies.

- **Easy to clean:** This air fryer comes with a removable non-stick coated drawer as well as a food basket. The non-stick coated drawer and food baskets are dishwasher safe. All it takes is to put it inside the dishwasher so that you don't have to spend time scrubbing and cleaning it to remove the dirt.

The Features of COSORI Air Fryer

If it is your first time to buy your COSORI Air Fryer, it is important that you know the things that are included in the box. When unboxing your COSORI Air Fryer, you will be able to get the following things such as the air fryer unit with the inner and outer frying basket, user manual, warranty card, and recipe book. The many benefits of COSORI Air Fryer are made possible thanks to the many features that this kitchen appliance has. Knowing the features of this particular air fryer is very important so that you will be able to optimize its use. Below are the features of the COSORI Air Fryer.

- **Wide temperature range:** The COSORI Air Fryer has a wide temperature range so that you will be able to cook different kinds of foods using this kitchen appliance. Its temperature range is from 180°F to 400°F with 10 degrees of increments. This feature allows you full and better control of your cooking. For instance, you can gently remove moisture from food at a lower temperature or make them crispy at high temperature. It comes with a °F and °C switch especially if you are not familiar with Fahrenheit. It also comes with a timer for 60 minutes.

- **Unique air circulation technology:** How food is cooked in an air fryer largely depends on what technology is used in this particular kitchen appliance. The COSORI Air Fryer uses a unique 360º Air Circulation Technology that uses fans that circulate heated air inside the air fryer's cooking tray. And since the tray basket allows the air to circulate evenly on all sides, this allows even cooking just as you would when you cook using a conventional fryer.

- **Pre-set built-in cooking settings:** What makes this air fryer unique compared to its many counterparts is that it comes with many built-in pre-set cooking settings. In fact, it is the only air fryer that has the most pre-set cooking options in the market. The touch screen menu features 11 pre-set cooking settings from Chicken, Steak, Shrimp, Seafood, Frozen Foods, Bacon, Vegetables, French Fries, Root Vegetables, Bread, and Desserts. With so many foods that can be cooked using this nifty kitchen appliance, it may replace other kitchen appliances altogether because of the many things that it can do.

- **Large capacity:** The COSORI Air Fryer has a basket size capacity of 5.8 quartz. This means that it can hold more than 5 liters of food. Unlike other air fryers, it is larger with a dimension of 13x14x11 inches and weight of 16.1 pounds. It basically can cook food for three to five people. Although heavy, it is still a perfect addition in your kitchen because you will no longer need to buy other kitchen appliances and kitchen equipment so you will have more space in your kitchen. The appliances and kitchen equipment that can be replaced by the COSORI Air Fryer include a conventional air fryer, several frying pans, an oven, indoor grill, and many others.

- **Attractive finish:** The COSORI Air Fryer is the air fryer of the future. It has a square design so it can fit any corners in the kitchen unlike the egg-shaped or round air fryers that are available in the market. Aside from its sleek design and intuitive digital display, it comes with a black brush matte finish thereby making it a perfect addition for conventional kitchens.

- **Dishwasher safe:** Although most parts of the COSORI Air Fryer contain electronics, parts such as the crisper drawer, air fryer basket, and other cooking accessories are dishwasher friendly. This saves time and trouble when it comes to cleaning the air fryer.

- **Intuitive safety features:** The safety features of this air fryer have been discussed deliberately earlier but it is crucial to discuss its myriad of safety features in this section. Aside from its auto shut-off function, it also comes with non-slip feet so that the kitchen appliance does not slide on the kitchen counter.

- **Comes with different accessories:** There are so many accessories that come with this particular kitchen appliance. The accessory kit that you can get for this air fryer includes a cake pan, metal holder, multipurpose rack with skewers, silicone mat, egg molds, and a pizza pan. These accessories are important as it allows you to optimize the use of your air fryer aside from merely frying different kinds of foods.

- **Warranty period:** The COSORI Air Fryer comes with at the most 2 years of limited warranty. This means that, in case you encounter problems with your air fryer, you can have them checked for free.

Limitations of The COSORI Air Fryer

Although the COSORI Air Fryer is considered as the best in the market it is important to take note that there are some limitations that you need to know. After all, there is no such thing as the perfect equipment.

One of the biggest limitations of the COSORI Air Fryer is that you cannot use metal utensils when cooking food.

However, what it lacks can be supplemented with the accessories that are included in the accessories kit. Moreover, people who are living by themselves may find this air fryer too big for them. However, there is a smaller version that has a capacity of 3.7 quarts but even this is too big for people who live by themselves.

Although this may be the case, you can still use this air fryer even if you are living by yourself to make big batches of meal prepped foods. Using the COSORI Air Fryer with meal prepping helps you prepare delicious meals in advance.

Chapter 2: General Instructions When Using Your COSORI Air Fryer

Now that you know about the features of your COSORI Air Fryer, it is important that you know how to use it so that you can optimize how you use it. Knowing how to use your COSORI Air Fryer will also help you make different kinds of food imaginable. Thus, below are tips on how you can use your COSORI Air Fryer.

- **Preheating gives crispier food:** Before using the COSORI Air Fryer, it is important to preheat it first for at least 5 minutes to improve the texture of the food. Although it may take a longer time to cook your food if you preheat it, your food will be crispier. But if you are wondering how long you need to preheat and what temperature to use, the COSORI Air Fryer comes with a preheat setting so that will set the temperature automatically. Once you press this preset button, the air fryer is kept at this mode until it reaches the decide temperature. Only then can you put your food inside.

- **Shake your food in the middle of cooking:** To cook food better, you need to shake the fryer basket halfway through the cooking time. This is especially true if you are using pre-set cooking settings such as Shrimps, French Fries, Frozen Foods, Vegetables, and Root Vegetables. You cannot forget it because when the pre-set cooking setting is in the middle of its cooking cycle beep five times. The beeps will serve as your reminder to shake your food. Shaking your food allows you to get better results.

- **Follow the recipes:** It is crucial to follow the recipes specific for COSORI Air Fryer so that you will come up with the best dishes using this nifty kitchen device. Since this air fryer comes with a 100-recipe booklet, it will be easier for you to cook many kinds of food. If, however, you are finished trying out all the recipes in the cookbook, there are many recipes that are available online. This book will also include great recipes that you can follow.

Using the Preset Air Frying Programs

Understanding how the pre-set cooking button works is very important so that you can cook food perfectly using your COSORI Air Fryer. The preset programs are programmed to cook food at ideal temperature and time. Below are the general steps when using pre-set cooking settings.

1.) Preheat the air fryer. It is important to take note that the higher the cooking temperature, the longer the preheat setting. You can refer to your manual for the different preheat settings available for your COSORI Air Fryer.

2.) Once the preheat temperature and time is achieved, the display will display the word "READY". This will be your cue to put your food in the basket.

3.) Choose the desired pre-set cooking program. You can also customize the temperature and cooking time by pressing the Press Temp/Time button once. Click on either the + or – button to adjust the temperature. To change the time, Press the Temp/Time button a second time and press the + or – button to change the time. You can only cook your food for a maximum of 60 minutes.

4.) Press the "Start" button to commence cooking. For some pre-set cooking settings, the Shake reminder will appear so be sure to flip the food halfway through the cooking time. Be careful of the hot steam when you take the cooking tray out. Do not press the Basket Release Button otherwise, the inner basket will fall. Once you are done flipping the food, put the basket back in the fryer.

5.) Once the food is cooked, press the Keep Warm button so that the food is kept warm until you are ready to eat your food.

It is important to take note that the different pre-set cooking settings work differently and although the instructions are the same for using the pre-set acids, their specific settings are different. Below is a table showing the differences between the different pre-set cooking settings found in your COSORI Air Fryer.

Pre-Set Setting	Symbol	Default Temperature (°F/°C)	Default Time (minutes)	Shake Reminder
Steak		400/205	6	-
Chicken		380/193	25	-
Seafood		350/177	8	-
Shrimp		370/188	6	Shake
Bacon		320/160	8	-
Frozen Food		350/177	10	Shake
French Fries		380/193	25	Shake
Vegetables		300/149	10	Shake
Root Veggies		400/205	12	Shake
Bread		320/160	12	-
Dessert		300/149	8	-
Preheat	PRE HEAT	400/205	5	-
Keep Warm	KEEP WARM	170/77	5	-

How to Do Manual Air Frying

If you want to cook your food without using any pre-set cooking time, you can still do manual air frying using the COSORI Air Fryer. The steps are still the same when using the pre-set cooking time except that you don't choose any pre-set cooking time. Below are the steps when doing manual air frying with your COSORI Air Fryer.

1.) Preheat your air fryer and wait for the screen to display "READY" before adding the food inside the fryer basket.

2.) Press the Temp/Time button once and adjust the temperature by pressing the + or – button to change the temperature.

3.) Press the Temp/Time button again and adjust the cooking time. Remember that you can only set the time between 1 and 60 minutes.

4.) Press the Start button to start cooking your food.

5.) Once the air fryer is done cooking your food, press the Keep Warm button.

General Safety Instructions

Now that you know how to use your COSORI Air Fryer, it is important that you know the general safety instructions so that you will be able to cook delicious foods using your air fryer without compromising your safety. The thing is that it is not enough that you rely on the safety features of your air fryer, but it is also critical that you follow the general safety instructions.

- **Do not fill with oil:** Never fill the air fryer with oil as it is not a deep fryer. Doing so may run the risk of overheating and burning your air fryer unit.

- **Do not press the button on the handle while shaking the basket:** This is especially true when you are shaking the contents of your hot air fryer basket. Pressing the handle of the air fryer basket will make the outer basket dislodge and it may accidentally injure you.

- **Never immerse your entire unit in water:** While the air fryer basket and tray are the only parts that you can put inside a dishwasher, never do the same thing for the entire unit because it houses all of the electrical components of the unit. If you need to clean the housing, use a moist sponge to wipe off dirt and clean the rest of the housing.

- **Never use third-party accessories and parts:** If you want to optimize your COSORI Air Fryer by buying accessories, it is crucial to take note that you should avoid getting third-party accessories because they may not be compatible and may cause premature damage to your air fryer.

COSORI Air Fryer Troubleshooting Guide

Your COSORI Air Fryer should work perfectly fine after unboxing them. However, if it does not work the first time, you need to know basic troubleshooting steps that you need to know.

Problem	Solutions
The air fryer will not turn on properly	- Make sure that that air fryer is plugged in correctly. - Push the basket tray properly into the air fryer.
Foods are not properly cooked	- Do not fill the entire basket with too much food. Allow some room for the air to flow - Increase the cooking temperature as well as time.
Foods are not cooked evenly	- The ingredients are stacked up on top and tightly packed inside the cooking tray. - Not shaking the food as recommended by the pre-set cooking button.
Foods are not crispy at all	- Spray or brush the surface of food with a little bit of oil to increase the crispiness
The basket does not slide properly in the air fryer	- Make sure that the basket is not filled with food to the brim. - If you are cooking a lot of food, cook in batches if possible
White smoke is coming out from the air fryer	- If you use it for the first time, your air fryer is bound to release white smoke. - Greasy food may also produce smoke and may leak out the outer basket. Make sure that you clean your entire unit properly.

Now that you know about the basics of the COSORI Air Fryer, you are ready to cook delicious foods using your air fryer. Read on so that you can try delicious air fryer recipes that are perfect for your COSORI Air Fryer. Enjoy!

Chapter 3: Breakfast & Brunch Recipes

Coconut Milk, Egg 'n Spinach Casserole
(Total Time: 20 Mins |Serves: 2)

Ingredients
- Salt and pepper to taste
- 6 large eggs, beaten
- 1 teaspoon garlic powder
- 1 tablespoon coconut oil
- 1 onion, chopped
- 1 ½ cups spinach, chopped and excess water squeezed out
- ¼ cup coconut milk

Instructions
1. Preheat the air fryer for 5 minutes.
2. In a mixing bowl, combine all ingredients except for the spinach and oil. Whisk until well-incorporated.
3. Rub oil all over a baking dish that fits your COSORI, spread spinach on bottom, and pour over the egg mixture.
4. Place in the air fryer chamber and cook for 20 minutes at 310°F.

Nutrition information:
Calories per serving: 376; Carbohydrates: 10.0g; Protein: 21.1g; Fat: 28.4g; Sugar: 4.0g; Sodium: 238mg; Fiber: 2.4g

Bell Pepper, Beef & Egg Scramble
(Total Time: 35 Mins |Serves: 4)

Ingredients
- Salt and pepper to taste
- 8 large eggs, beaten
- 3 cloves of garlic, minced
- 1-pound ground beef, 85% lean
- 1 onion, chopped
- 1 green bell pepper, seeded and chopped

Instructions
1. Preheat the air fryer at 400°F.
2. In a baking dish that fits your COSORI mix the ground beef, onion, garlic, olive oil, and bell pepper. Season with salt and pepper to taste.
3. Place dish in COSORI and cook for 10 minutes.
4. Open the air fryer, mix and crumble beef well.
5. Pour in the beaten eggs and give a good stir.
6. Continue cooking for 25 minutes at 330°F.

Nutrition information:
Calories per serving: 431; Carbohydrates: 6.2g; Protein: 42.8g; Fat: 25.9g; Sugar: 2.7g; Sodium: 260mg; Fiber: 0.9g

Spanish Rice Casserole with Cheesy Beef

(Total Time: 50 Mins |Serves: 2)

Ingredients

- 2 tablespoons chopped green bell pepper
- 1/4 teaspoon Worcestershire sauce
- 1/4 teaspoon ground cumin
- 1/4 cup shredded Cheddar cheese
- 1/4 cup finely chopped onion
- 1/4 cup chile sauce
- 1/3 cup uncooked long grain rice
- 1/2-pound lean ground beef
- 1/2 teaspoon salt
- 1/2 teaspoon brown sugar
- 1/2 pinch ground black pepper
- 1/2 cup water
- 1/2 (14.5 ounce) can canned tomatoes
- 1 tablespoon chopped fresh cilantro

Instructions

1. Preheat COSORI to 360ºF.
2. Lightly grease a dish that fits in your COSORI Air fryer with cooking spray. Add ground beef. Pop in the air fryer and cook for 10 minutes. Halfway through cooking time, stir and crumble beef. Discard excess fat,
3. Stir in pepper, Worcestershire sauce, cumin, brown sugar, salt, chile sauce, rice, water, tomatoes, green bell pepper, and onion. Mix well. Cover dish with foil and cook for 25 minutes. Stirring occasionally.
4. Give it one last good stir, press down firmly and sprinkle cheese on top.

5. Cook uncovered for 15 minutes at 390°F until tops are lightly browned.
6. Serve and enjoy with chopped cilantro.

Nutrition information:

Calories per serving: 460; Carbohydrates: 35.8g; Protein: 37.8g; Fat: 17.9g; Sugar: 6.7g; Sodium: 1040mg; Fiber: 3g

Marinara Sauce Over Cheesy Eggplant Bake

(Total Time: 45 Mins |Serves: 4)

Ingredients

- salt and freshly ground black pepper to taste
- 2 tablespoons shredded pepper jack cheese
- 1-1/2 teaspoons olive oil
- 1-1/2 cups prepared marinara sauce
- 1/4 teaspoon red pepper flakes
- 1/4 cup water, plus more as needed
- 1/4 cup grated Parmesan cheese
- 1/4 cup grated Parmesan cheese
- 1/4 cup and 2 tablespoons ricotta cheese
- 1/4 cup and 2 tablespoons dry breadcrumbs
- 1/2 pinch salt, or as needed
- 1 tablespoon olive oil
- 1 tablespoon olive oil
- 1 large eggplant
- 1 clove garlic, sliced

Instructions

1. Cut eggplant crosswise in 5 pieces. Peel and chop two pieces into ½-inch cubes.
2. Lightly grease a dish that fits your COSORI Air fryer with 1 tbsp olive oil. For 5 minutes, heat oil at 390°F. Add half eggplant strips and cook for 2 minutes per side. Transfer to a plate.
3. Add 1 ½ tsp olive oil and garlic. Cook for a minute. Add chopped eggplants. Season with pepper flakes and salt. Cook for 4 minutes.

Lower heat to 330ºF and continue cooking eggplants until soft, around 8 minutes more.
4. Stir in water and marinara sauce. Cook for 8 minutes until heated through. Stirring every now and then. Transfer to a bowl.
5. In a bowl, whisk well pepper, salt, pepper jack cheese, Parmesan cheese, and ricotta. Evenly spread cheeses over eggplant strips and then fold in half.
6. Lay folded eggplant in same dish. Pour marinara sauce on top.
7. In a small bowl whisk well olive oil, and breadcrumbs. Sprinkle all over sauce.
8. Cook for 15 minutes at 390ºF until tops are lightly browned.
9. Serve and enjoy.

Nutrition information:

Calories per serving: 269; Carbohydrates: 23.4g; Protein: 9.9g; Fat: 15.8g; Sugar: 8.5g; Sodium: 386mg; Fiber: 5.6g

Garlic 'n Sour Cream Zucchini Bake

(Total Time: 20 Mins |Serves: 3)

Ingredients

- 1/4 cup grated Parmesan cheese
- paprika to taste
- 1 tablespoon minced garlic
- 1 large zucchini, cut lengthwise then in half
- 1 cup sour cream
- 1 (8 ounce) package cream cheese, softened

Instructions

1. Lightly grease a dish that fits in your COSORI Air fryer with cooking spray.
2. Place zucchini slices in a single layer in dish.
3. In a bowl whisk well, remaining Ingredients: except for paprika. Spread on top of zucchini slices. Sprinkle paprika.
4. Cover dish with foil.
5. For 10 minutes, cook on 390ºF.
6. Remove foil and cook for 10 minutes at 330ºF.
7. Serve and enjoy.

Nutrition information:

Calories per serving: 385; Carbohydrates: 13.5g; Protein: 11.9g; Fat: 32.4g; Sugar: 5.5g; Sodium: 553mg; Fiber: 1.1g

Smoked Trout Frittata

(Total Time: 15 Mins |Serves: 4)

Ingredients
- Salt and pepper to taste
- 6 eggs, beaten
- 2 tablespoons olive oil
- 2 tablespoons coconut oil
- 2 fillets smoked trout, shredded
- 1 onion, chopped

Instructions
1. Preheat the air fryer for 5 minutes.
2. Place all ingredients in a mixing bowl until well-combined.
3. Pour into a baking dish that will fit in the air fryer.
4. Cook for 15 minutes at 400°F.

Nutrition information:

Calories per serving: 283; Carbohydrates: 3.1g; Protein: 17.0g; Fat: 22.5g; Sugar: 1.4g; Sodium: 117mg; Fiber: 0.5g

Bacon-Spinach Egg Cups

(Total Time: 10 Mins | Serves: 4)

Ingredients
- Salt and pepper to taste
- 4 eggs, beaten
- 3 tablespoons butter
- 1 bacon strip, fried and crumbled
- ¼ cup spinach, chopped finely

Instructions
1. Preheat the air fryer to 350°F.
2. In a mixing bowl, combine the eggs, butter, and spinach. Season with salt and pepper to taste.
3. Grease 4 ramekins with cooking spray and evenly pour the egg mixture into ramekins.
4. Sprinkle with bacon bits.
5. Place the ramekins in the air fryer. If needed, cook in batches.
6. Cook for 10 minutes.

Nutrition information:
Calories per serving: 148; Carbohydrates: 1.5g; Protein: 6.0g; Fat: 13.2g; Sugar: 0.7g; Sodium: 84mg; Fiber: 0.2g

Chives, Coconut Cream & Mushroom Quiche

(Total Time: 20 Mins |Serves: 4)

Ingredients

- Salt and pepper to taste
- 4 eggs, beaten
- 2 tablespoons coconut oil
- 1 tablespoon chives, chopped
- ½ onion, chopped
- ½ cup mushroom, sliced
- ½ cup almond flour
- ¼ cup coconut cream

Instructions

1. Preheat the air fryer to 350°F.
2. In a mixing bowl, combine the almond flour and coconut oil.
3. Press the almond flour mixture at the bottom of a heat-proof baking dish.
4. Place in the air fryer and cook for 5 minutes.
5. Meanwhile, combine the rest of the ingredients in a mixing bowl.
6. Pour over the egg mixture on the baked crust.
7. Continue cooking for 15 minutes or until eggs have set.

Nutrition information:

Calories per serving: 250; Carbohydrates: 6.3g; Protein: 9.0g; Fat: 22.2g; Sugar: 1.9g; Sodium: 65mg; Fiber: 2.2g

Zucchini 'n Chorizo Frittata

(Total Time: 15 Mins | Serves: 2)

Ingredients

- A dash of Spanish paprika
- A dash of oregano
- 3 large eggs, beaten
- 1 tablespoon olive oil
- ½ zucchini, sliced
- ½ chorizo sausage, sliced

Instructions

1. Preheat the air fryer to 350°F.
2. Combine all ingredients in a mixing bowl until well-incorporated.
3. Pour into a greased baking dish that will fit in the air fryer basket.
4. Place the baking dish in the air fryer.
5. Close and cook for 15 minutes.

Nutrition information:

Calories per serving: 235; Carbohydrates: 0.9g; Protein: 13.1g; Fat: 19.6g; Sugar: 0.3g; Sodium: 292mg; Fiber: 0g

Creamy Ham 'n Egg Casserole

(Total Time: 15 Mins |Serves: 4)

Ingredients
- Salt and pepper to taste
- 4 large eggs, beaten
- 3 slices uncured ham, chopped
- 2 teaspoon fresh chives, chopped
- 2 tablespoons coconut cream
- 2 tablespoons butter, unsalted
- 1 egg, whole

Instructions
1. Preheat the air fryer to 350°F.
2. In a mixing bowl, combine the beaten eggs, coconut cream, butter, and chives. Season with salt and pepper to taste.
3. Pour into a baking dish that will fit in the air fryer and sprinkle ham on top.
4. Crack 1 egg on top.
5. Place in the air fryer and Cook for 15 minutes.

Nutrition information:
Calories per serving: 185; Carbohydrates: 2.2g; Protein: 11.1g; Fat: 14.8g; Sugar: 0.8g; Sodium: 309mg; Fiber: 0.3g

Garlic Beef & Egg Brekky Frittata

(Total Time: 20 Mins |Serves: 4)

Ingredients

- Salt and pepper to taste
- 3 eggs, beaten
- 3 cloves of garlic, minced
- 1 tablespoon olive oil
- 1 onion, chopped
- ½ pound ground beef

Instructions

1. Preheat the air fryer to 400°F.
2. Place a dish inside air fryer basket, and grease with oil. Add onion and garlic. Cook for 3 minutes.
3. Add beef and cook for 10 minutes. Stirring halfway through cooking time.
4. In a mixing bowl, combine the rest of the ingredients
5. Once beef is done cooking, crumble and evenly spread on bottom of dish. Por egg mixture on top.
6. Cook for 20 minutes at 320°F.

Nutrition information:

Calories per serving: 240; Carbohydrates: 4.6g; Protein: 19.1g; Fat: 15.7g; Sugar: 1.9g; Sodium: 87mg; Fiber: 0.7g

Creamy Mushroom-Egg Bake

(Total Time: 20 Mins |Serves: 4)

Ingredients

- Salt and pepper to taste
- 8 eggs, beaten
- 2 tablespoons butter
- 1 teaspoon onion powder
- 1 cup coconut cream
- ½ cup mushrooms, chopped

Instructions

1. Preheat the air fryer to 320°F.
2. In a mixing bowl, combine the eggs, butter, and coconut cream.
3. Pour in a baking dish together with the mushrooms and onion powder.
4. Season with salt and pepper to taste.
5. Place in the air fryer chamber and cook for 20 minutes.

Nutrition information:

Calories per serving: 384; Carbohydrates: 6.6g; Protein: 14.0g; Fat: 35.0g; Sugar: 1.2g; Sodium: 175mg; Fiber: 1.7g

Chapter 4: Appetizers & Sides Recipes

Paprika, Garlic 'n Onion Rubbed Chicken Strips
(Total Time: 25 Mins | Serves: 6)

Ingredients
- 1 cup coconut milk
- 1 tablespoon cayenne pepper
- 1 teaspoon garlic powder
- 1 teaspoon onion powder
- 1-pound chicken breast, cut into strips
- 2 cups almond flour
- 2 eggs
- 2 tablespoons paprika
- Salt and pepper to taste

Instructions
1. Season the chicken meat with salt and pepper to taste. Set aside.
2. In a mixing bowl, combine the eggs and coconut milk. Set aside.
3. In another bowl, mix the almond flour, paprika, garlic powder, and onion powder.
4. Preheat COSORI Air fryer to 350°F.
5. Soak the chicken meat in the egg mixture then dredge in the flour mixture.
6. Place in the air fryer basket and cook for 25 minutes, flipping once after 15-minutes of cooking time has elapsed. If needed, cook in batches.
7. Meanwhile, prepare the hot sauce by combining the cayenne pepper and vegetable.

8. Serve sauce on the side once chicken is cooked.

Nutrition information:
Calories per serving: 221; Carbohydrates: 5.5g; Protein: 20.6g; Fat: 13.6g; Sugar: 2.1g; Sodium: 64mg; Fiber: 2.2g

Crispy Fried Chicken Breasts Buffalo Style

(Total Time: 30 Mins | Serves: 6)

Ingredients

- ¼ cup sugar-free hot sauce
- ¼ teaspoon cayenne pepper
- ¼ teaspoon paprika
- 1 clove of garlic, minced
- 1 cup almond flour
- 1 large egg, beaten
- 1 teaspoon stevia powder
- 1-pound chicken breasts, cut into thick strips
- 3 tablespoons butter
- Salt and pepper to taste

Instructions

1. Preheat the air fryer to 350°F.
2. Slice chicken into 6 strips. Season with salt and pepper to taste.
3. In one bowl, beat eggs and season lightly with salt. In another bowl, whisk well almond flour and season lightly with pepper and salt.
4. Dredge first chicken in beaten egg then in flour mixture.
5. Arrange neatly in the air fryer basket.
6. Close and cook for 30 minutes. Flip after 20-minutes of cooking time has elapsed.
7. Meanwhile, prepare the sauce by combining the rest of the ingredients. Season the sauce with salt and pepper to taste. Set aside.
8. Once the chicken tenders are cooked, place in a bowl with the sauce and toss to coat.

Nutrition information:

Calories per serving: 289; Carbohydrates: 4.5g; Protein: 20.5g; Fat: 21.5g; Sugar: 1.1g; Sodium: 110mg; Fiber: 2.2g

Zucchini Garlic Fries

(Total Time: 15 Mins | Serves: 6)

Ingredients
- ¼ teaspoon garlic powder
- ½ cup almond flour
- 2 large egg whites, beaten
- 3 medium zucchinis, sliced into fry sticks
- Salt and pepper to taste

Instructions
1. Preheat the air fryer to 400°F.
2. Mix all ingredients in a bowl until the zucchini fries are well coated.
3. Place in the air fryer basket.
4. Close and cook for 15 minutes for 400°F. Shaking basket halfway through cooking time.

Nutrition information:
Calories per serving: 11; Carbohydrates: 1.1g; Protein: 1.5g; Fat: 0.1g; Sugar: 0.5g; Sodium: 19mg; Fiber: 0.2g

Paprika 'n Cajun Seasoned Onion Rings

(Total Time: 20 Mins |Serves: 6)

Ingredients
- ¼ cup coconut milk
- ½ teaspoon Cajun seasoning
- ¾ cup almond flour
- 1 ½ teaspoon paprika
- 1 large white onion
- 1 teaspoon garlic powder
- 2 large eggs, beaten
- Salt and pepper to taste

Instructions
1. Preheat COSORI Air fryer to 400°F.
2. Peel the onion, cut off the top and slice into circles.
3. In a mixing bowl, combine the coconut milk and the eggs.
4. Soak the onion in the egg mixture.
5. In another bowl, combine the almond flour, paprika garlic powder, Cajun seasoning, salt and pepper.
6. Dredge the onion in the almond flour mixture.
7. Place in the air fryer.
8. Cook for 12 minutes and shake halfway thru. Cook in two batches.

Nutrition information:
Calories per serving: 62; Carbohydrates: 3.9g; Protein: 2.8g; Fat: 4.1g; Sugar: 1.6g; Sodium: 44mg; Fiber: 0.9g

Crab Cakes Seasoned with Old Bay 'n Dijon

(Total Time: 15 Mins |Serves: 6)

Ingredients

- Salt and pepper to taste
- 2 large eggs
- 1-pound lump crab meat
- 1 teaspoon Worcestershire sauce
- 1 teaspoon Dijon mustard
- 1 ½ teaspoon old bay seasoning
- ½ cup panko
- ¼ cup chopped green onion

Instructions

1. Preheat the air fryer to 390°F.
2. In a mixing bowl, combine all ingredients until everything is well-incorporated.
3. Use your hands to form small patties of crab cakes.
4. Place on the air fryer basket and cook for 15 minutes.
5. Flip the crab cakes halfway through the cooking time for even browning.

Nutrition information:

Calories per serving: 128; Carbohydrates: 7.8g; Protein: 17.0g; Fat: 2.7g; Sugar: 1.2g; Sodium: 535mg; Fiber: 0.6g

Coconut Shrimps with Pina Colada Dip

(Total Time: 20 Mins |Serves: 8)

Ingredients
- Toasted coconut meat for garnish
- Salt and pepper to taste
- 2/3 cup coconut milk
- 2 tablespoons honey
- 1/3 cup non-fat Greek yogurt
- 1/3 cup light coconut milk
- 1 cup shredded coconut flakes
- 1 ½ pounds jumbo shrimps, peeled and deveined
- ¾ cups panko breadcrumbs
- ½ cup cornstarch
- ¼ cup pineapple chunks, drained

Instructions
1. Preheat the air fryer to 390°F.
2. Place the shrimps and cornstarch in a Ziploc bag and give a good shake.
3. In a bowl, stir in coconut milk and honey. Set aside.
4. In another bowl, mix the coconut flakes and breadcrumbs. Set aside.
5. Dip the shrimps in the milk mixture then dredge in the breadcrumbs.
6. Place in COSORI Air fryer and cook for 10 minutes. Shaking after 7 minutes has elapsed. Cook in two batches
7. Meanwhile, combine the rest of the Ingredients to create the dipping sauce.

Nutrition information:

Calories per serving: 293; Carbohydrates: 25.3g; Protein: 21.9g; Fat: 11.8g; Sugar: 12.2g; Sodium: 866mg; Fiber: 2.1g

Crispy Paprika-Fish Nuggets

(Total Time: 25 Mins | Serves: 8)

Ingredients
- Salt and pepper to taste
- 2 eggs, beaten
- 2 cloves of garlic, minced
- 1 teaspoon smoked paprika
- 1 teaspoon chili powder
- 1 tablespoon olive oil
- 1 tablespoon lemon juice
- 1 cup almond flour
- 1 ½ pounds fresh fish fillet, chopped finely

Instructions
1. Place all ingredients in a bowl and mix until well-combined.
2. Form small nuggets using your hands. Place in the fridge to set for 2 hours.
3. Preheat the air fryer to 350°F.
4. Carefully place the nuggets in the fryer basket. Cook in two batches.
5. Cook each batch for 12 minutes, shaking basket after 7 minutes has elapsed.

Nutrition information:
Calories per serving: 164; Carbohydrates: 3.9g; Protein: 17.1g; Fat: 9.1g; Sugar: 0.9g; Sodium: 284mg; Fiber: 1.8g

Buffalo Chicken Dip

(Total Time: 20 Mins |Serves: 8)

Ingredients

- 1 (8 ounce) package cream cheese, softened
- 1 tablespoon shredded pepper Jack cheese
- 1/2 pinch cayenne pepper, for garnish
- 1/2 pinch cayenne pepper, or to taste
- 1/4 cup and 2 tablespoons hot pepper sauce (such as Frank's Reshoot®)
- 1/4 cup blue cheese dressing
- 1/4 cup crumbled blue cheese
- 1/4 cup shredded pepper Jack cheese
- 1/4 teaspoon seafood seasoning (such as Old Bay®)
- 1-1/2 cups diced cooked rotisserie chicken

Instructions

1. Lightly grease a dish that fits in your COSORI Air fryer with cooking spray. Mix in cayenne pepper, seafood seasoning, crumbled blue cheese, blue cheese dressing, pepper Jack, hot pepper sauce, cream cheese, and chicken.
2. For 15 minutes, cook on 390°F.
3. Let it stand for 5 minutes and garnish with cayenne pepper.
4. Serve and enjoy.

Nutrition information:

Calories per serving: 248.5; Carbohydrates: 4.0g; Protein: 21.1g; Fat: 16.7g; Sugar: 2.1g; Sodium: 697mg; Fiber: 0.2g

Chapter 5: Poultry Recipes

Garlic Rosemary Roasted Cornish Hen
(Total Time: 45 Mins |Serves: 2)

Ingredients
- 1 tsp rosemary
- 1 whole Cornish game hen
- 4 cloves of garlic, minced
- Salt and pepper to taste

Instructions
1. Season the whole chicken with garlic, salt, and pepper.
2. Place in the air fryer basket.
3. Cook for 30 minutes at 330°F.
4. Flip the chicken in the other side and cook for another 15 minutes.

Nutrition information:

Calories per serving: 166; Carbohydrates: 4.2g; Protein: 26.5g; Fat: 4.3g; Sugar: 1.2g; Sodium: 72mg; Fiber: 0.5g

Ginger-Garam Masala Rubbed Chicken

(Total Time: 50 Mins |Serves: 8)

Ingredients

- 2 tablespoons olive oil
- 1 whole chicken, sliced into 8 pieces
- 1 thumb-size ginger, grated
- 1 teaspoon turmeric powder
- 1 teaspoon garam masala
- 1 teaspoon coriander powder
- 1 cup coconut milk
- 1 bell pepper, seeded and julienned

Instructions

1. Preheat the air fryer to 350°F.
2. Place all ingredients in a baking dish that will fit in the air fryer.
3. Stir to combine.
4. Place in the air fryer.
5. Cook for 50 minutes. Halfway through cooking time, turnover chicken pieces and stir to mix.

Nutrition information:

Calories per serving: 236; Carbohydrates: 2.7g; Protein: 25.1g; Fat: 13.8g; Sugar: 1.3g; Sodium: 95mg; Fiber: 0.9g

Delicious Chicken Cordon Bleu

(Total Time: 30 Mins | Serves: 2)

Ingredients
- ¼ cup almond flour
- 1 slice cheddar cheese
- 1 slice of ham
- 1 small egg, beaten
- 1 teaspoon parsley
- 2 chicken breasts, butterflied
- Salt and pepper to taste

Instructions
1. Season the chicken with parsley, salt and pepper to taste.
2. Place the cheese and ham in the middle of the chicken and roll. Secure with toothpick.
3. Soak the rolled-up chicken in egg and dredge in almond flour.
4. Place in the air fryer.
5. Cook for 30 minutes at 350°F. Turnover chicken after 20 minutes of cooking time.

Nutrition information:
Calories per serving: 458; Carbohydrates: 5.3g; Protein: 64.1g; Fat: 19.1g; Sugar: 1.8g; Sodium: 394mg; Fiber: 1.8g

Southern Style Fried Chicken

(Total Time: 35 Mins |Serves: 2)

Ingredients
- 2-pcs chicken leg quarters
- 1 teaspoon salt
- 1 teaspoon pepper
- 1 teaspoon paprika
- 1 teaspoon garlic powder
- ½ cup coconut flour

Instructions
1. Preheat the air fryer to 350°F.
2. Combine all ingredients in a bowl, except for chicken. Give a good stir.
3. Add chicken and cover well with batter.
4. Place chicken in the air fryer.
5. Cook for 35 minutes. After 20 minutes, turnover chicken.

Nutrition information:

Calories per serving: 321; Carbohydrates: 27.7g; Protein: 32.6g; Fat: 8.3g; Sugar: 1.4g; Sodium: 1704mg; Fiber: 1.7g

Chicken Marinated in Coconut Milk with Ginger-Cilantro

(Total Time: 25 Mins |Serves: 4)

Ingredients
- Salt and pepper to taste
- 1-pound chicken tenders, cut in half
- 1 teaspoon turmeric
- 1 teaspoon smoked paprika
- 1 teaspoon garam masala
- 1 tablespoon minced garlic
- 1 tablespoon grated ginger
- ½ cup coconut milk
- ¼ cup cilantro leaves, chopped

Instructions
1. Place all ingredients in a bowl and stir to coat the chicken with all ingredients.
2. Allow to marinate in the fridge for 2 hours.
3. Preheat the air fryer to 400°F.
4. Place the chicken pieces in the air fryer basket.
5. Cook for 25 minutes at 400°F. Turnover chicken pieces after 17 minutes has elapsed.

Nutrition information:
Calories per serving: 173; Carbohydrates: 3.7g; Protein: 24.0g; Fat: 6.8g; Sugar: 1.2g; Sodium: 90mg; Fiber: 1.0g

Turkey Meatballs in Cranberry Sauce

(Total Time: 25 Mins | Serves: 4)

Ingredients

- 2 teaspoons cider vinegar
- 1-pound ground turkey
- 1/4-pound ground bacon
- 1/3 cup cranberry sauce
- 1 tsp salt and more to taste
- 1 1/2 tablespoons barbecue sauce
- 1 ½ tablespoons water

Instructions

1. In a bowl, mix well with hands the turkey, ground bacon and a tsp of salt. Evenly form into 16 equal sized balls.
2. In a small saucepan boil cranberry sauce, barbecue sauce, water, cider vinegar, and a dash or two of salt. Mix well and simmer for 3 minutes.
3. Preheat COSORI Air fryer to 360°F.
4. For 15 minutes cook meatballs and shake basket halfway through cooking time.
5. Pour sauce over cooked meatballs, serve and enjoy.

Nutrition information:

Calories per serving: 329; Carbohydrates: 11.7g; Protein: 25.9g; Fat: 19.9g; Sugar: 11.0g; Sodium: 853mg; Fiber: 0.3g

Creamy Chicken Breasts Bake

(Total Time: 25 Mins | Serves: 4)

Ingredients
- ¼ cup olive oil
- 1 block cream cheese
- 2 chicken breasts
- 8 slices of bacon, fried and crumbled
- Salt and pepper to taste

Instructions
1. Preheat the air fryer for 5 minutes.
2. Place the chicken breasts in a baking dish that will fit in the air fryer.
3. Add the olive oil and cream cheese. Season with salt and pepper to taste.
4. Place the baking dish with the chicken and cook for 25 minutes at 350°F.
5. Sprinkle crumbled bacon after.

Nutrition information:
Calories per serving: 557; Carbohydrates: 3.4g; Protein: 35.7g; Fat: 44.2g; Sugar: 2.6g; Sodium: 970mg; Fiber: 0.2g

Hearty Chicken Potpie

(Total Time: 30 Mins |Serves: 4)

Ingredients

- Salt and pepper to taste
- 2 eggs
- 2 cloves of garlic, minced
- 2 ½ tablespoons butter, melted
- 1-pound ground chicken
- 1/3 cup coconut flour
- 1 tablespoon butter
- 1 cup chicken broth
- ¾ cup coconut milk
- ½ cup broccoli, chopped
- ¼ small onion, chopped

Instructions

1. Preheat the air fryer to 325°F.
2. Place 1 tablespoon butter, broccoli, onion, garlic, coconut milk, chicken broth, and ground chicken in a baking dish that will fit in the air fryer. Season with salt and pepper to taste.
3. In a mixing bowl, combine the 2.5 tablespoons butter, coconut flour, and eggs.
4. Sprinkle evenly the top of the chicken and broccoli mixture with the coconut flour dough.
5. Place the dish in the air fryer.
6. Cook for 30 minutes at 325°F.

Nutrition information:

Calories per serving: 436; Carbohydrates: 6.3g; Protein: 26.3g; Fat: 35.0g; Sugar: 3.1g; Sodium: 427mg; Fiber: 1.6g

Butter-Lemon on Chicken Thighs

(Total Time: 35 Mins | Serves: 4)

Ingredients

- 1/2 cup almond flour
- ½ cup chicken stock
- 1 egg, beaten
- 1 small onion, diced
- 1-pound chicken thighs
- 2 tablespoons capers
- 1 tablespoon olive oil
- 2 tablespoons butter
- Juice from 1 lemon, freshly squeezed
- Salt and pepper to taste

Instructions

1. Preheat the air fryer to 325°F.
2. Combine all ingredients in a baking dish. Make sure that all lumps are removed.
3. Place the baking dish in the air fryer chamber.
4. Cook for 35 minutes at 325°F. After 25 minutes of cooking time, turnover chicken pieces and mix sauce well.

Nutrition information:

Calories per serving: 391; Carbohydrates: 5.4g; Protein: 22.4g; Fat: 30.9g; Sugar: 2.3g; Sodium: 309mg; Fiber: 0.7g

Garlicky-Dijon Chicken Thighs

(Total Time: 25 Mins | Serves: 4)

Ingredients

- Salt and pepper to taste
- 2 teaspoons herbs de Provence
- 2 tablespoon olive oil
- 1-pound chicken thighs
- 1 tablespoon Dijon mustard
- 1 tablespoon cider vinegar

Instructions

1. Place all ingredients in a Ziploc bag.
2. Allow to marinate in the fridge for at least 2 hours.
3. Preheat the air fryer to 350°F.
4. Place the chicken in the fryer basket.
5. Cook for 25 minutes at 350°F. After 15 minutes of cooking, turnover thighs.

Nutrition information:

Calories per serving: 318; Carbohydrates: 1.6g; Protein: 19.1g; Fat: 25.7g; Sugar: 0.6g; Sodium: 136mg; Fiber: 0.3g

Chapter 6: Beef, Pork and Lamb Recipes

Honey-Balsamic Sauce on Roast Beef
(Total Time: 1.5 Hrs|Serves: 2)

Ingredients
- 2 cloves of garlic, minced
- 1-pound boneless roast beef
- 1 teaspoon coconut aminos
- 1 tablespoons olive oil
- 1 tablespoon Worcestershire sauce
- 1 tablespoon honey
- 1 cup beef organic beef broth
- ½ teaspoon red pepper flakes
- ¼ cup balsamic vinegar

Instructions
1. Place all ingredients in a baking dish and make sure that the entire surface of the beef is coated with the spices.
2. Place the baking dish with the beef in the air fryer.
3. Cover top with foil.
4. Cook for 1 hour and 15 minutes at 300ºF.
5. Remove foil and cook at 400ºF for 15 minutes more.

Nutrition information:
Calories per serving: 554; Carbohydrates: 18.2g; Protein: 61.3g; Fat: 26.1g; Sugar: 15.1g; Sodium: 735mg; Fiber: 0.3g

Homemade Corned Beef with Onions

(Total Time: 50 Mins | Serves: 4)

Ingredients
- Salt and pepper to taste
- 1 cup water
- 1-pound corned beef brisket, cut into chunks
- 1 tablespoon Dijon mustard
- 1 small onion, chopped

Instructions
1. Preheat the air fryer to 400°F.
2. Place all ingredients in a baking dish that will fit in the air fryer.
3. Cover with foil.
4. Cook for 35 minutes.
5. Remove foil, mix well, turnover beef, and continue cooking for another 15 minutes.

Nutrition information:
Calories per serving: 238; Carbohydrates: 3.1g; Protein: 17.2g; Fat: 17.1g; Sugar: 1.3g; Sodium: 1427mg; Fiber: 0.6g

Southwestern Meaty Pasta Bake

(Total Time: 45 Mins | Serves: 4)

Ingredients

- 2 garlic cloves, minced
- 1-pound lean ground beef
- 1/2 teaspoon pepper
- 1/2 teaspoon ground cumin
- 1/2 can (6 ounces) tomato paste
- 1/2 can (4 ounces) chopped green chilies, drained
- 1/2 can (16 ounces) kidney beans, rinsed and drained
- 1 teaspoons salt
- 1 teaspoon chili powder
- 1 large onion, chopped
- 1 jalapeno pepper, seeded and chopped
- 1 cup uncooked elbow macaroni, cooked according to manufacturer's instructions
- 1 cup shredded Monterey Jack cheese
- 1 can (14-1/2 ounces each) diced tomatoes, undrained

Instructions

1. Lightly grease a dish that fits in your COSORI Air fryer with cooking spray. Add ground beef, onion, and garlic. For 10 minutes, cook on 360ºF. Halfway through cooking time, stir and crumble beef.
2. Mix in diced tomatoes, kidney beans, tomato paste, green chilies, salt, chili powder, cumin, and pepper. Mix well. Cook for another 10 minutes.
3. Stir in macaroni and mix well. Top with jalapenos and cheese.
4. Cover dish with foil.

5. Cook for 15 minutes at 390°F, remove foil and continue cooking for another 10 minutes until tops are lightly browned.
6. Serve and enjoy.

Nutrition information:
Calories per serving: 453; Carbohydrates: 29.7g; Protein: 36.5g; Fat: 21.0g; Sugar: 7.5g; Sodium: 1048mg; Fiber: 5.6g

BBQ Memphis Pork Ribs

(Total Time: 35 Mins |Serves: 2)

Ingredients

- 1-pound pork spareribs
- 1 tablespoon salt
- 1 tablespoon dark sugar
- 1 tablespoon sweet paprika
- 1 teaspoon garlic powder
- 1 teaspoon poultry seasoning
- ½ cup apple juice
- ½ teaspoon mustard powder
- ½ teaspoon ground black pepper

Instructions

1. Place all ingredients in a mixing bowl and mix until everything is combined.
2. Allow to marinate in the fridge for at least 2 hours.
3. Preheat the air fryer to 330°F.
4. Place the pork spareribs in air fryer and cook for 30 minutes.
5. Meanwhile, put the marinade in a saucepan and allow to simmer for 10 minutes until reduced.
6. Brush the spareribs with the sauce, cook for 5 minutes more.
7. Serve and enjoy with extra sauce as dip.

Nutrition information:

Calories per serving: 885; Carbohydrates: 15.6g; Protein: 48.5g; Fat: 70.6g; Sugar: 10.9g; Sodium: 3715mg; Fiber: 1.8g

Chinese Salt and Pepper Pork

(Total Time: 40 Mins | Serves: 4)

Ingredients

- 4 pork chops
- 2 tablespoons toasted sesame seeds
- 2 green bell peppers, chopped
- 1 teaspoon sesame oil
- 1 teaspoon Chinese five-spice powder
- 1 red bell pepper, chopped
- 1 egg white, beaten
- ¾ cup potato starch
- ½ teaspoon sea salt

Instructions

1. Preheat the air fryer to 330°F.
2. Season the pork chops with salt and five spice powder.
3. Dip in egg white and dredge in potato starch.
4. Place in the air fryer basket and cook for 20 minutes. Turnover after 12 minutes has elapsed. Cook in two batches.
5. Meanwhile, heat oil in a skillet and stir-fry the bell peppers.
6. Serve the bell peppers on top of pork chops and garnish with sesame seeds.

Nutrition information:

Calories per serving: 401; Carbohydrates: 9.3g; Protein: 43.1g; Fat: 20.5g; Sugar: 2.0g; Sodium: 419mg; Fiber: 1.8g

Spicy Breaded Air Fried Pork Chops

(Total Time: 40 Mins |Serves: 4)

Ingredients

- 4 boneless pork chops
- Salt and pepper to taste
- 1 large egg, beaten
- ½ cup panko breadcrumbs
- 1/3 cup cornflakes crumbs
- 2 tablespoons parmesan cheese
- 1 ¼ teaspoon paprika
- ½ teaspoon garlic powder
- ½ teaspoon onion powder
- ¼ teaspoon chili powder

Instructions

1. Preheat the air fryer to 390ºF.
2. Season the pork chops with salt and pepper to taste.
3. Put beaten egg in a bowl. Set aside.
4. In another bowl, combine the rest of the ingredients.
5. Dip the pork in egg and dredge in flour mixture.
6. Place in the air fryer and cook for 20 minutes until crispy. Once 12 minutes has elapsed, turnover chops and continue cooking. Coo in two batches.

Nutrition information:

Calories per serving: 288; Carbohydrates: 6.2g; Protein: 43.9g; Fat: 8.5g; Sugar: 1.1g; Sodium: 180mg; Fiber: 0.8g

Grilled Beef with Soy-Daikon Sauce

(Total Time: 15 Mins |Serves: 2)

Ingredients
- Salt and pepper to taste
- 2 strip steaks
- 1 tablespoon olive oil
- ½ cup soy sauce
- ½ cup rice wine vinegar
- ¼ cup grated daikon radish

Instructions
1. Preheat the air fryer to 390°F.
2. Season the steak with salt and pepper.
3. Brush with oil.
4. for 15 minutes and make sure to flip the beef halfway through the cooking time.
5. Prepare the dipping sauce by combining the soy sauce and vinegar.
6. Serve the steak with the sauce and daikon radish.

Nutrition information:
Calories per serving: 520; Carbohydrates: 19.3g; Protein: 54.5g; Fat: 24.1g; Sugar: 14.2g; Sodium: 1135mg; Fiber: 1.9g

Sage 'n Thyme Rubbed Porterhouse

(Total Time: 30 Mins | Serves: 2)

Ingredients
- ¼ cup fish sauce
- 2 porterhouse steaks
- 2 tablespoons marjoram
- 2 tablespoons sage
- 2 tablespoons thyme
- Salt and pepper to taste

Instructions
1. Place all ingredients in a Ziploc bag and allow to marinate in the fridge for at least 2 hours.
2. Preheat the air fryer to 400°F.
3. Cook one side for 10 minutes, flip and cook the other side for another 10 minutes. Cook in batches.

Nutrition information:
Calories per serving: 1178; Carbohydrates: 6.3g; Protein: 112.5g; Fat: 75.5g; Sugar: 2.6g; Sodium: 3086mg; Fiber: 2.2g

Cheesy-Bacon Stuffed Pastry Pie

(Total Time: 18 Mins |Serves: 3)

Ingredients

- 1/2 cup bacon, cooked
- 1/2 cup cheddar cheese, shredded
- 1/2 cup sausage crumbles, cooked
- 5 eggs
- one box puff pastry sheets

Instructions

1. Scramble the eggs and cook.
2. Lightly grease a dish that fits in your COSORI Air fryer with cooking spray.
3. Evenly spread half of the puff sheets on bottom of dish.
4. Spread eggs, cooked sausage, crumbled bacon, and cheddar cheese.
5. Top with remaining puff pastry and gently push down with a fork.
6. Cover top of dish with foil.
7. For 8 minutes, cook on 330°F. Remove foil and continue cooking for another 5 minutes or until tops of puff pastry is golden brown.
8. Serve and enjoy.

Nutrition information:

Calories per serving: 359; Carbohydrates: 9.5g; Protein: 18.0g; Fat: 28.0g; Sugar: 0.4g; Sodium: 656mg; Fiber: 0.9g

Sweet 'n Sour Glazed Meatloaf

(Total Time: 40 Mins |Serves: 3)

Ingredients

- 8-oz tomato sauce, divided
- 5 Tbsp Heinz reduced-sugar ketchup
- 3 tsp Splenda (or Truvia) brown sugar blend
- 1-pound lean ground beef (93% fat free), raw
- 1-2 tsp salt
- 1-2 tsp freshly ground black pepper
- 1/3 cup Kellogg's corn flakes crumbs
- 1 tsp dried basil
- 1 tsp (or 2 cloves) minced garlic
- 1 Tbsp Worcestershire sauce
- ½ Tbsp lightly dried (or fresh chopped) Parsley
- ½ medium onion, chopped

Instructions

1. Lightly grease a dish that gits in your COSORI Air fryer with cooking spray.
2. In a large bowl, mix well 6-oz tomato sauce, garlic, pepper, salt, corn flake crumbs, and onion. Stir in ground beef and mix well with hands.
3. Evenly spread ground beef mixture in dish, ensuring that it is lumped altogether.
4. In a medium bowl, whisk all remaining ingredients together to make a glaze. Pour on top of ground beef.
5. Cover dish with foil.
6. For 20 minutes, cook on 340°F. Remove foil and continue cooking for another 15 minutes.

7. Let it stand for 5 minutes.
8. Serve and enjoy.

Nutrition information:
Calories per serving: 494; Carbohydrates: 37.6g; Protein: 43.6g; Fat: 17.2g; Sugar: 18.7g; Sodium: 2642mg; Fiber: 5.5g

Jambalaya with Shrimps 'n Sausage

(Total Time: 40 Mins |Serves: 4)

Ingredients
- salt to taste
- 1-1/2 teaspoons olive oil
- 1-1/2 teaspoons minced garlic
- 1-1/2 bay leaves
- 1/8 teaspoon dried thyme leaves
- 1/4-pound smoked sausage, cut into 1/4-inch thick slices
- 1/4 teaspoon Cajun seasoning, or to taste
- 1/2 pound peeled and deveined medium shrimp (30-40 per pound)
- 1/2 large onion, chopped
- 1/2 cup uncooked white rice
- 1/2 cup chopped green bell pepper
- 1/2 cup chopped celery
- 1/2 (14.5 ounce) can diced tomatoes with juice
- 1 cup chicken broth

Instructions
1. Lightly grease a baking pan that fits in your COSORI Air fryer with olive oil. Add sausage and for 5 minutes, cook on 360°F. Stir in Cajun seasoning, salt, celery, bell pepper, and onion. Cook for another 5 minutes.
2. Add the rice and mix well. Stir in thyme leaves, bay leaves, chicken broth, garlic, vegetable mixture, and tomatoes with juice. Cover with foil.
3. Cook for another 15 minutes.
4. Remove foil, stir in shrimp. Cook for 8 minutes.

5. Let it stand for 5 minutes.
6. Serve and enjoy.

Nutrition information:
Calories per serving: 226; Carbohydrates: 26.1g; Protein: 15.3g; Fat: 7.0g; Sugar: 2.1g; Sodium: 906mg; Fiber: 2.5g

Mexican Rice 'n Sausage Bake

(Total Time: 45 Mins |Serves: 4)

Ingredients

- 2/3 cup uncooked long grain white rice
- 1/4-pound Cheddar cheese, shredded
- 1-1/3 cups water
- 1/2-pound ground pork breakfast sausage
- 1/2 (16 ounce) jar picante sauce
- 1/2 (8 ounce) container sour cream

Instructions

1. Ring water to a boil in a saucepan and stir in rice. Cover and simmer for 20 minutes until all liquid is absorbed. Turn off fire and fluff rice.
2. Lightly grease baking pan that fits in your COSORI Air fryer with cooking spray. Add sausage and cook for 10 minutes at 360ºF. Halfway through cooking time, crumble and stir sausage.
3. Stir in cooked rice, sour cream, and picante sauce. Mix well. Sprinkle cheese on top
4. Cook for 15 minutes at 390ºF until tops are lightly browned.
5. Serve and enjoy.

Nutrition information:

Calories per serving: 361; Carbohydrates: 32.2g; Protein: 16.5g; Fat: 18.2g; Sugar: 6.2g; Sodium: 1219mg; Fiber: 2.2g

Cheesy Bacon Burger Casserole

(Total Time: 35 Mins |Serves: 6)

Ingredients

- 8-ounces frozen Tater Tots
- 6 bacon strips, cooked and crumbled
- 4-ounces process cheese (Velveeta)
- 1-pound ground beef
- 1/4 cup sliced dill pickles
- 1/2 cup shredded cheddar cheese
- 1/2 cup grape tomatoes, chopped
- 1/2 can (15 ounces) tomato sauce
- 1 tablespoon Worcestershire sauce
- 1 tablespoon ground mustard
- 1 small onion, chopped

Instructions

1. Lightly grease baking pan that fits in your COSORI Air fryer with cooking spray. Add beef and half of onions.
2. For 10 minutes, cook on 390°F. Halfway through cooking time, stir and crumble beef.
3. Stir in Worcestershire, mustard, Velveeta, and tomato sauce. Mix well. Cook for 4 minutes until melted.
4. Mix well and evenly spread in pan. Top with cheddar cheese and then bacon strips.
5. Evenly top with tater tots. Cover pan with foil.
6. Cook for 15 minutes at 390°F. Uncover and bake for 10 minutes more until tops are lightly browned.
7. Serve and enjoy topped with pickles and tomatoes and remaining onion.

Nutrition information:
Calories per serving: 397; Carbohydrates: 15.1g; Protein: 29.5g; Fat: 24.1g; Sugar: 4.2g; Sodium: 890mg; Fiber: 1.6g

Mouthwatering Beef Potpie Recipe

(Total Time: 45 Mins |Serves: 4)

Ingredients

- Salt and pepper to taste
- 3/4-pound ground beef
- 2 tablespoons coconut oil
- 2 cloves of garlic, minced
- 2 beaten eggs
- 1 yellow bell pepper, julienned
- 1 tablespoon butter
- 1 red bell pepper, julienned
- 1 onion, chopped
- 1 green bell pepper, julienned
- 1 cup almond flour

Instructions

1. Preheat the air fryer to 330ºF.
2. In a baking dish that will fit in the air fryer, spread coconut oil all over the dish surface.
3. In a bowl, with hands mix pepper, salt, garlic, beef, bell peppers, onion, and ground beef. Mix well and then place on oiled dish.
4. Place butter on top in slices.
5. In a mixing bowl, mix the almond flour and eggs to create a dough.
6. Press the dough over the beef mixture.
7. Place in the air fryer and cook for 35 minutes at 320ºF.
8. Increase heat to 370ºF and continue cooking for another 10 minutes.

Nutrition information:

Calories per serving: 365; Carbohydrates: 7.5g; Protein: 25.6g; Fat: 25.8g; Sugar: 3.6g; Sodium: 116mg; Fiber: 1.2g

Chapter 7: Vegan and Vegetarian Recipes

Seasoned Veggie Wontons
(Total Time: 20 Mins |Serves: 4)

Ingredients
- Water for sealing wontons
- Salt to taste
- 30 wonton wrappers
- 2 tablespoons olive oil
- 1 teaspoon garlic powder
- 1 tablespoon chili sauce
- ¾ cup grated cabbage
- ¾ cup chopped red pepper
- ½ teaspoon white pepper
- ½ cup grated white onion
- ½ cup grated carrots
- ½ cup chopped mushrooms

Instructions
1. In a skillet over medium heat, place all vegetables and cook until all moisture has been released from the vegetables.
2. Remove from the heat and season with chili sauce, garlic powder, white pepper, and salt.
3. Put wonton wrapper on a working surface and add a tablespoon of the vegetable mixture in the middle of the wrapper. Wet the edges of the wonton wrapper with water and fold the wrapper to close and securely seal in the veggies.
4. Brush with oil and place in the air fryer basket.

5. Close the air fryer and cook for 10 minutes at 330ºF per batch.

Nutrition information:
Calories per serving: 287; Carbohydrates: 44.4g; Protein: 7.4g; Fat: 8.9g; Sugar: 3.0g; Sodium: 461mg; Fiber: 3.1g

Veggie Burger with Spice Medley

(Total Time: 30-45 Mins |Serves: 4)

Ingredients

- salt and pepper to taste
- 3 tablespoon plain flour
- 2 teaspoons thyme
- 2 teaspoons parsley
- 2 teaspoons garlic, minced
- 2 teaspoons coconut oil melted
- 2 teaspoons chives
- 1 teaspoon mustard powder
- 1 flax egg (1 flaxseed egg + 3 tablespoon water)
- 1 cup breadcrumbs
- ½ pound cauliflower, steamed and diced
- ½ cup oats
- ¼ cup desiccated coconut

Instructions

1. Preheat the air fryer to 390°F.
2. Place the cauliflower in a tea towel and ring out excess water. Place in a mixing bowl and add all ingredients except the breadcrumbs. Mix well until well combined.
3. Form 8 burger patties with the mixture using your hands.
4. Roll the patties in breadcrumbs and place in the air fryer basket. Make sure that they do not overlap. If needed cook in batches.
5. Cook for 10 to 15 minutes or until the patties are crisp.

Nutrition information:

Calories per serving: 130; Carbohydrates: 20.7g; Protein: 6.2g; Fat: 4.8g; Sugar: 2.2g; Sodium: 146mg; Fiber: 3.6g

Bell Pepper-Mushroom Pizza

(Total Time: 10 Mins |Serves: 2)

Ingredients

- salt and pepper
- 1 vegan pizza dough
- 1 shallot, julienned
- 1 cup mushrooms, sliced thinly
- ½ red bell pepper, julienned
- ¼ tsp Italian seasoning
- ¼ cup pizza sauce
- ¼ cup cheese

Instructions

1. Preheat the air fryer to 400°F.
2. Slice the pizza dough into squares. Set aside.
3. In a mixing bowl, mix together the oyster mushroom, shallot, bell pepper and parsley.
4. Season with salt and pepper to taste.
5. Place the topping on top of the pizza squares.
6. Place inside the air fryer and cook for 10 minutes. If needed, cook in batches.

Nutrition information:

Calories per serving: 222; Carbohydrates: 26.0g; Protein: 8.8g; Fat: 9.4g; Sugar: 3.8g; Sodium: 238mg; Fiber: 1.8g

Creamy Baked Potato with Olives

(Total Time: 40 Mins | Serves: 2)

Ingredients

- a dollop of vegan cream cheese
- a dollop of vegan butter
- 1/8 teaspoon salt
- 1 teaspoon olive oil
- 1 tablespoon Kalamata olives
- 1 tablespoon chives, chopped
- 1 medium russet potato, scrubbed and peeled
- ¼ teaspoon onion powder

Instructions

1. Place inside the air fryer basket and cook for 40 minutes at 400°F. Be sure to turn the potatoes once halfway.
2. Place the potatoes in a mixing bowl and pour in olive oil, onion powder, salt, and vegan butter.
3. Serve the potatoes with vegan cream cheese, Kalamata olives, chives, and other vegan toppings that you want.

Nutrition information:

Calories per serving: 318; Carbohydrates: 34.4g; Protein: 5.2g; Fat: 18.7g; Sugar: 1.7g; Sodium: 352mg; Fiber: 2.6g

Middle Eastern Falafel Recipe

(Total Time: 15 Mins | Serves: 4)

Ingredients

- cooking spray
- 3 tablespoons all-purpose flour
- 3 cloves garlic
- 2 cups chickpeas from can, drained and rinsed
- 1 teaspoon cumin seeds
- 1 tablespoon juice from freshly squeezed lemon
- ½ teaspoon salt
- ½ teaspoon red pepper flakes
- ½ teaspoon coriander seeds
- ½ onion, diced
- ¼ cup parsley, chopped
- ¼ cup coriander, chopped

Instructions

1. In a skillet over medium heat, toast the cumin and coriander seeds until fragrant.
2. Place the toasted seeds in a mortar and grind the seeds.
3. In a food processor, place all ingredients except for the cooking spray. Add the toasted cumin and coriander seeds.
4. Pulse until fine.
5. Shape the mixture into round patties and spray cooking oil.
6. Place inside a 400°F preheated air fryer and make sure that they do not overlap. If needed, cook in two batches.
7. Cook for 15 minutes or until the surface becomes golden brown.

Nutrition information:

Calories per serving: 217; Carbohydrates: 37.7g; Protein: 10.4g; Fat: 3.5g; Sugar: 6.2g; Sodium: 565mg; Fiber: 8.9g

Garlicky Kale-Potato Nuggets
(Total Time: 20 Mins | Serves: 2)

Ingredients
- cooking spray
- 4 cups kale, rinsed and chopped
- 2 cups boiled potatoes, finely chopped
- 1/8 teaspoon black pepper
- 1/8 cup almond milk
- 1 teaspoon extra-virgin olive oil
- 1 clove of garlic, minced
- ¼ teaspoon salt

Instructions
1. Preheat the air fryer to 400°F.
2. Place a foil at the base of the air fryer basket and poke holes to allow air circulation.
3. Heat oil in a large skillet and sauté the garlic for 2 minutes. Add the kale until it wilts. Transfer to a large bowl.
4. Add the potatoes and almond milk. Season with salt and pepper to taste.
5. Form balls and spray with cooking oil.
6. Place inside the air fryer and cook for 20 minutes or until golden brown.

Nutrition information:
Calories per serving: 183; Carbohydrates: 36.6g; Protein: 4.3g; Fat: 2.9g; Sugar: 3.4g; Sodium: 322mg; Fiber: 4.2g

Milky-Sauce on Cauliflower Steak

(Total Time: 15 Mins |Serves: 2)

Ingredients
- salt and pepper to taste
- 2 tablespoons onion, chopped
- 1 tablespoon olive oil
- 1 cauliflower, sliced into two
- ¼ teaspoon vegetable stock powder
- ¼ cup almond milk

Instructions
1. Soak the cauliflower in salted water or brine for at least 2 hours.
2. Preheat the air fryer to 400°F.
3. Rinse the cauliflower and place inside the air fryer and cook for 15 minutes.
4. Meanwhile, heat oil in a skillet over medium flame. Sauté the onions and stir until translucent. Add the vegetable stock powder and milk.
5. Bring to boil and adjust the heat to low.
6. Allow the sauce to reduce and season with salt and pepper.
7. Place cauliflower steak on a plate and pour over sauce.

Nutrition information:

Calories per serving: 161; Carbohydrates: 20.5g; Protein: 6.4g; Fat: 8.0g; Sugar: 9.8g; Sodium: 114mg; Fiber: 6.5g

Pesto-Cream Cheese Stuffed Mushrooms

(Total Time: 15 Mins |Serves: 4)

Ingredients

- Salt to taste
- 1-pound cremini mushrooms, stalks removed
- 1 tablespoon lemon juice, freshly squeezed
- 1 cup basil leaves
- ½ cup pine nuts
- ½ cup cream cheese
- ¼ cup olive oil

Instructions

1. Place all ingredients except the mushrooms in a food processor.
2. Pulse until fine.
3. Scoop the mixture and place on the side where the stalks were removed.
4. Place the mushrooms in the fryer basket.
5. Close and cook for 15 minutes in a 350°F preheated air fryer.

Nutrition information:

Calories per serving: 347; Carbohydrates: 7.9g; Protein: 6.8g; Fat: 34.0g; Sugar: 4.6g; Sodium: 180mg; Fiber: 2.1g

Cheesy-Bacon Stuffed Jalapeno

(Total Time: 30 Mins |Serves: 4)

Ingredients

- Salt to taste
- 4-ounce cream cheese
- 16 strips of uncured bacon, cut into half
- 16 fresh jalapenos, sliced lengthwise and seeded
- 1 teaspoon paprika
- ¼ cup cheddar cheese, shredded

Instructions

1. In a mixing bowl, mix together the cream cheese, cheddar cheese, salt, and paprika until well-combined.
2. Scoop half a teaspoon onto each half of jalapeno peppers.
3. Use a thin strip of bacon and wrap it around the cheese-filled jalapeno half. Wear gloves when doing this step because jalapeno is very spicy.
4. Place in the air fryer basket and cook for 15 minutes in a 350°F preheated air fryer. Cook in two batches.

Nutrition information:

Calories per serving: 280; Carbohydrates: 26.1g; Protein: 9.2g; Fat: 17.8g; Sugar: 15.9g; Sodium: 512mg; Fiber: 10.8g

Easy-Peasy Balsamic Brussels Sprouts

(Total Time: 15 Mins |Serves: 2)

Ingredients
- ¼ teaspoon salt
- 1 tablespoon balsamic vinegar
- 2 cups Brussels sprouts, halved
- 2 tablespoons olive oil

Instructions
1. Preheat the air fryer to 350°F.
2. Mix all ingredients in a bowl until the Brussels sprouts are well coated.
3. Place in the air fryer basket.
4. Close and cook for 15 minutes and shake basket halfway through cooking time.

Nutrition information:
Calories per serving: 164; Carbohydrates: 9.2g; Protein: 3.0g; Fat: 13.8g; Sugar: 3.1g; Sodium: 315mg; Fiber: 3.3g

Chapter 8: Desserts Recipes

Mouthwatering Blackberry Cobbler
(Total Time: 20 Mins |Serves: 6)

Ingredients
- 3/4 cup white sugar
- 3 cups fresh blackberries
- 2 tablespoons melted butter
- 2 tablespoons melted butter
- 1-1/4 cups all-purpose flour
- 1-1/2 teaspoons vanilla extract
- 1-1/2 teaspoons baking powder
- 1/4 cup white sugar
- 1/2 teaspoon salt
- 1 tablespoon cornstarch
- 1 cup milk

Instructions
1. Lightly grease baking pan of air fryer with cooking spray. Add blackberries and drizzle with 2 tbsps. melted butter.
2. In a small bowl, whisk cornstarch and 1/4 cup sugar. Sprinkle over blackberries and toss well to coat.
3. In another bowl, whisk well salt, baking powder, and ¾ cup sugar. Stir in 2 tbsps. melted butter, vanilla, and milk. Mix well and pour over berries.
4. For 20 minutes, cook on 390°F or until tops are lightly browned.
5. Serve and enjoy.

Nutrition information:
Calories per serving: 308; Carbohydrates: 53.8g; Protein: 3.7g; Fat: 9.5g; Sugar: 38.9g; Sodium: 274mg; Fiber: 4.2g

Blueberry-Lemon Cake

(Total Time: 17 Mins |Serves: 6)

Ingredients

- 1/4 cup avocado oil (or any light cooking oil)
- 2 1/2 cups self-rising flour
- 1/2 cup Monk Fruit (or use your preferred sugar)
- 1/2 cup cream
- 2 eggs
- 1 cup blueberries
- zest from 1 lemon
- juice from 1 lemon
- 1 tsp. vanilla
- brown sugar for topping (a little sprinkling on top of each muffin—less than a teaspoon)

Instructions

1. In mixing bowl, beat well wet Ingredients. Stir in dry ingredients and mix thoroughly.
2. Lightly grease baking pan of air fryer with cooking spray. Pour in batter.
3. For 12 minutes, cook on 330°F.
4. Let it stand in air fryer for 5 minutes.
5. Serve and enjoy.

Nutrition information:

Calories per serving: 348; Carbohydrates: 45.1g; Protein: 7.7g; Fat: 15.0g; Sugar: 4.7g; Sodium: 656mg; Fiber: 2.0g

Garlic-Parmesan Knots

(Total Time: 16 Mins |Serves: 12)

Ingredients
- Garlic salt
- 3 tbsp Olive oil
- 3 tbsp Minced garlic
- 1 13.8-oz refrigerated pizza crust
- ¼ cup Parmesan cheese, grated

Instructions
1. Roll dough out onto a cutting board. Cut dough into equal ¼-inch strips. Wrap each strip into knots
2. Mix olive oil & garlic in a bowl. Dip each knot into the mixture.
3. Lightly grease baking pan of air fryer with cooking spray. Add knots in a single layer and cook in batches for 4 minutes at 390°F.
4. Dust with Parmesan.
5. Serve and enjoy.

Nutrition information:
Calories per serving: 145; Carbohydrates: 11.0g; Protein: 4.6g; Fat: 9.3g; Sugar: 1.4g; Sodium: 254mg; Fiber: 0.8g

Tasty Peach Pies

(Total Time: 24 Mins | Serves: 8)

Ingredients
- 3 tablespoons granulated sugar
- 2 (5-oz.) fresh peaches, peeled and chopped
- 1/4 teaspoon table salt
- 1 teaspoon vanilla extract
- 1 teaspoon cornstarch
- 1 tablespoon fresh lemon juice (from 1 lemon)
- 1 (14.1-oz.) pkg. refrigerated piecrusts

Instructions
1. In medium bowl, whisk well salt, vanilla, sugar, and lemon juice. Let stand for 15 minutes while stirring every now and then. Drain while reserving a tablespoon of the liquid.
2. In reserved liquid mix in cornstarch and then stir into drained peaches.
3. Slice crusts into 8 pieces of 4-inch circles. Add a tablespoon of peach filling. Brush sides of dough with water, fold in half and crimp edge with fork to seal dough. Repeat to remaining doughs.
4. Lightly grease air fryer basket with cooking spray. Add dough in a single layer and cook in batches.
5. For 8 minutes, cook on 390ºF.
6. Serve and enjoy.

Nutrition information:
Calories per serving: 282; Carbohydrates: 36.1g; Protein: 2.0g; Fat: 14.4g; Sugar: 6.0g; Sodium: 309mg; Fiber: 1.2g

Churros with Choco Dip

(Total Time: 30 Mins |Serves: 12)

Ingredients

- 1/2 cup (about 2 1/8 oz.) all-purpose flour
- 1/4 teaspoon kosher salt
- 1/4 cup, plus 2 Tbsp. unsalted butter, divided
- 1/3 cup granulated sugar
- 1/2 cup water
- 2 large eggs
- 2 teaspoons ground cinnamon
- 4 ounces bittersweet baking chocolate, finely chopped
- 3 tablespoons heavy cream
- 2 tablespoons vanilla kefir

Instructions

1. In small saucepan, bring to a boil ¼ cup butter, salt, and water. Stir in flour and lower fire to a simmer. Cook until smooth and thickened and pulls away from side of pan.
2. Transfer dough to a bowl and stir constantly until cooled.
3. Stir in eggs one at a time.
4. Transfer to a pastry bag with a star tip. Chill for half an hour.
5. Lightly grease baking pan of air fryer with cooking spray. Pipe dough on bottom of pan in 3-inch lengths.
6. For 10 minutes, cook on 390oF. Halfway through cooking time, shake. Cook in batches
7. In a small bowl mix cinnamon and sugar. In another bowl, place melted butter.
8. Brush cooked churros with melted butter and then roll in sugar mixture.

9. In microwave safe bowl, melt cream and chocolate. Mix well and stir in vanilla.
10. Serve and enjoy with dip on the side.

Nutrition information:

Calories per serving: 160; Carbohydrates: 10.2g; Protein: 3.0g; Fat: 11.4g; Sugar: 3.2g; Sodium: 65mg; Fiber: 1.9g

Salted Pistachios on Brownies
(Total Time: 25 Mins |Serves: 4)

Ingredients
- 1/4 cup nondairy milk
- 1/4 cup aquafaba
- 1/2 teaspoon vanilla extract
- 1/2 cup whole wheat pastry flour
- 1/2 cup vegan sugar
- 1/4 cup cocoa powder
- 1 tablespoon ground flax seeds
- 1/4 teaspoon salt

Instructions
1. In a large bowl, whisk well all dry ingredients. Beat in the wet ingredients until combined thoroughly.
2. Lightly grease a baking pan that fits in your COSORI Air fryer with cooking spray. Pour in batter and evenly spread.
3. For 20 minutes, cook on preheated 330°F air fryer.
4. Let it sit for 5 minutes.
5. Serve and enjoy.

Nutrition information:
Calories per serving: 130; Carbohydrates: 27.7g; Protein: 3.8g; Fat: 2.1g; Sugar: 13.2g; Sodium: 155mg; Fiber: 3.7g

Made in the USA
Coppell, TX
13 July 2025

51829364R00052